PENGUIN
BLOOM

PENGUIN
BLOOM

Young Readers' Edition

**By Chris Kunz, based on the screenplay
by Shaun Grant & Harry Cripps**

ABC
BOOKS

The ABC 'Wave' device is a trademark of the
Australian Broadcasting Corporation and is used
under licence by HarperCollins*Publishers* Australia.

HarperCollins*Publishers*
Australia • Brazil • Canada • France • Germany • Holland • Hungary
India • Italy • Japan • Mexico • New Zealand • Poland • Spain
Sweden • Switzerland • United Kingdom • United States of America

First published in Australia in 2021
by HarperCollins*Children's Books*
a division of HarperCollins*Publishers* Australia Pty Limited
Level 13, 201 Elizabeth Street, Sydney NSW 2000, Australia
ABN 36 009 913 517
harpercollins.com.au

Text by Chris Kunz, from a screenplay by Shaun Grant and Harry Cripps,
based on *Penguin Bloom* by Cameron Bloom and Bradley Trevor Greive

A catalogue record for this book is available
from the National Library of Australia

ISBN 978 0 7333 4167 0 (paperback)
ISBN 978 1 4607 1369 3 (ebook)

Cover images by Joel Pratley
Cover images copyright © Penguin Bloom Film Holdings Pty Ltd 2021
Typeset in Sabon LT Std by Kirby Jones
Printed and bound in Australia by McPherson's Printing Group
The papers used by HarperCollins in the manufacture of this book
are a natural, recyclable product made from wood grown in sustainable
plantation forests. The fibre source and manufacturing processes meet
recognised international environmental standards, and carry certification.

My dad fell in love with Mum while eating a pie. Her parents owned a bakery on the coast and when she wasn't studying at uni, she worked behind the counter. Dad memorised the days she worked just so he could see her. He said she was stubborn, fearless and cute.

Dad wasn't so interested in studying. He loved surfing and photography. He told me he'd picked up his father's old camera when he was thirteen years old, and from that moment on knew exactly what he wanted to do with his life. And when he met Mum, he knew exactly who he wanted to spend his life with.

One day, after a surf, he worked up the courage to let Mum ask him out. And that was it. Dad's first, last and only girlfriend. They married in their backyard, and then went all the way to Kenya for their honeymoon.

My parents have always loved to travel, even when they didn't have much money. And they did a lot of travel before us kids were born. They went back to Africa five times before we turned up.

I was first. My name's Noah. When Mum realised I was ready to come out, she rode with Dad to the hospital on their beloved silver Vespa. The hospital staff couldn't believe it.

Rueben was annoying from before he was even born. You know what little brothers are like. Mum had to be cut open so the doctors could drag him out, kicking and screaming. Some things never change.

And then Oli was born, lucky last. He was really

cute as a baby, smiling and giggling and making us all laugh. That hasn't changed either.

The story I'm about to tell you is the story of us. My dad, Cameron, my mum, Sam, and their three boys — Noah (me), Rueben and Oli. We're the Blooms. We live by the beach on the Northern Beaches of Sydney, in Australia. We all love the ocean and spend as much time there as we can, swimming and surfing.

I guess we all kinda knew our life was perfect and that we wouldn't change a thing.

But sometimes you don't get that choice, do you? Sometimes stuff happens that you would do anything to try to avoid. But you can't. And that's what happened to us.

Oh, and I should definitely mention that this story is also about a scared little magpie chick who fell out of her nest on a stormy night.

There are parts of our story I'm not going to enjoy telling you, and there are parts that I didn't know at the time, but Mum and Dad talked to me about them later. Because we all believe it's the sort of story that needs to be told.

So I should just get started, shouldn't I?

CHAPTER 1

We weren't a family that had done a lot of travel overseas before we went to Thailand. We mainly stayed at home, spending time at the beach and with family. Which suited us just fine. But Mum and Dad had itchy feet and wanted to show us firsthand how amazing travel could be. They had been working hard and saving up their money for a long time so the five of us could jump on an aeroplane and visit Asia for the first time.

Thailand is a ten-hour plane ride away from Australia, and it turns out that is a really long time to sit still if you're the kind of kids who like to skate, bike, surf and play football as much as we Blooms did.

But we got there eventually, and Phuket was great. Really different to what we were used to in Australia. There were markets and throngs of people and spicy food and strong smells and fireworks and lots of tourists. It was busy and energetic, and did I mention how many tourists there were? Mum and Dad were keen to spend time in a place that was more 'off the beaten track' as they put it, so we jumped on a local bus and headed north.

Dad had given me one of his old digital cameras, and I loved taking videos of the world outside the bus window. There were jungles and mountains and lots of busy Thai people going about their lives as we passed by.

We spent the first night in a small coastal town with hardly any tourists, and when we woke the next day, we had the beach to ourselves. It was perfect. There were swaying coconut palms, breaking waves, hot sun and the Blooms on holiday. We swam, we wrestled, we dived, and Dad took photos of Mum teaching us how to split a coconut cleanly in half.

I will be honest here. Although Rueben and I were convinced we would be professional coconut crackers — Rueben thought he'd be better than me, of course (he wasn't) — it turned out we needed more practice. Oli's coconut remained pretty much untouched, even though he yelled at it to split, and mine and Rueben's broke into pieces. Mum's, on the other hand, split perfectly in two.

Luckily Mum was willing to share the juice from her perfect coconut with us all, and like baby birds, we lined up as she poured the juice into our mouths. It was the freshest coconut juice we'd ever drunk.

Then there was more body-surfing, and swimming races with Mum, because she is a *very* competitive lady. She likes to win, and when she decides she's going to do something, she's going to do it really,

really well. And Dad is her biggest champion. He cheers her on, taking photos all the time.

There was hugging, general clowning around and too much kissing between Mum and Dad, but us kids didn't mind (although we splashed them when they didn't stop kissing after two seconds). This was turning out to be the best family holiday ever. Or so we thought.

*

We were planning to hire some bikes and go for a ride in the afternoon, and we saw a viewing platform near the hotel we were staying in. It was only two storeys high, but it would give us a good view of the surrounding area. So we thought we should go up and have a look, decide which direction we were going to bike in.

As usual, Dad was taking pictures of us boys and we were goofing around. And that's when things went horribly wrong. I was looking out at the beach when I heard a really awful clanging noise. Mum had been leaning against a railing near the edge of the viewing platform, enjoying the sunshine, but now that railing was broken. And there was no sign of Mum. It didn't make sense. I looked over at Dad and he seemed frozen, his camera clasped to his chest. Time slowed down. My brain couldn't process what I was seeing. One moment Mum was there and the next she had disappeared.

I don't know how much time passed before Dad rushed to the edge of the viewing platform and looked down. He made a terrible noise that didn't sound like it had come from a human being at all.

And then he raced down the stairs, yelling for help.

CHAPTER 2

So our perfect family holiday turned into a nightmare in two seconds. Mum had fallen and was really seriously injured. We weren't sure if she was going to live or die, but none of us could imagine a life without her, so we decided she was going to have to live.

And luckily for us, she did. But it wasn't easy. She'd fallen onto concrete paving below the viewing platform and she had a lot of injuries. She had broken her back in what the doctors call T6 but what Mum calls her bra strap. She can't feel anything from there down except for when she has the hiccups. She had also cracked her head, causing a temporary brain injury, which made her lose her sense of taste. If all that wasn't bad enough, many of her internal organs had also been damaged. She was taken by ambulance to a hospital in Thailand and operated on, and then, when it was considered safe for her to fly, she travelled back to Sydney and went straight to a hospital there. More surgeries followed, and physiotherapy and more waiting, but eventually the doctors decided she was healed and didn't need to be in hospital any longer.

When she finally came home, we were so happy to have her back with us. But by then we knew she wouldn't be able to walk again, and our always-active, always-hardworking, full-of-love-and-energy mum would now have a different life. We were all scared for her.

And she was scared for herself. She didn't know how to be Sam Bloom anymore. Things that you never had to think about, like how easy it was to climb out of bed in the morning, were a hundred times more difficult when you couldn't move your own legs. She had to use a big wooden stick to lever herself out of bed, and it was really hard to do. Because she'd been in hospital for so long, the muscles she'd always had from her busy outdoor life had gone, and it was like she was a baby again, learning to do basic things.

Dad was amazing. He did everything he could to keep the household running and to keep everyone's spirits up, even though sometimes we were ratbag kids who would rather play handball in the living room than help out with Mum.

My favourite place to be in those days was on our rooftop. I know that sounds dangerous, but let me explain. Our roof is completely flat — it's basically a big rectangular space where we can look out over the valley and beach. We've even set up skateboard ramps up there. It's also where we keep our beehives. Our rooftop is like another room of our house, the sunniest one and with the best view.

There's a built-in ladder at the back of the house, so it's easy to climb up and down. Oh, and I should mention the trampoline in the front yard. Because if there are no adults around, you can do a run-up from the top of the roof and jump off, landing on the trampoline. Rueben did it all the time.

I liked to spend time by myself on the rooftop. To avoid my brothers and their bickering about nothing, I'd grab my breakfast and head up to the roof to hang out with the bees, who, even on their buzziest days, were quieter than my brothers. I enjoyed the time away from all that was happening inside the house.

But poor Dad couldn't do everything by himself, and he'd often ask me to help out, coming out of the house and looking up to the roof, trying not to sound too tired and frustrated.

'Bit of help needed down here. Come on, mate!'

I just wasn't sure how to help. I wanted Mum to get her old life back, and I knew I couldn't help her do that. Instead, I'd watch as Dad carefully helped her to the bathroom. She now had a large red scar down her spine. I could tell how much pain she was in, and I knew she didn't want me to know, so she would smile and say hi to me, and I would say hi back, trying to smile but not making eye contact. Maybe it only looked like a sad grimace.

In the kitchen one morning, Oli was dressed in his school uniform, and Rueben had tied Oli's feet to a skateboard with footy socks. He was standing on the skateboard, ready to launch.

'Is this going to hurt again?' Oli asked.

'Not if you land properly,' said Rueben, which was far from the truth. Poor Oli was Rueben's willing guinea pig, always trusting Rueben and often ending up with bruises and scratches from all the experiments gone wrong. Oli loved every moment of it.

'On your marks. Get set …' Rueben pushed Oli out of the kitchen, into a couple of Mum's access ramps that my brothers had made into jumps in the middle of the hallway. Oli launched, getting some impressive air, but unsurprisingly stacked it on landing. Oli and Rueben laughed. 'Sick!'

Oli was checking his elbows for new bruises. There was one or two, nothing major, but worth pointing out to his friends at school at recess.

Mum rolled into the hallway, her wet hair tucked under a grey beanie. The wheelchair couldn't get past the ramps. She was stuck. 'Boys?' she said, trying to hide her frustration.

Dad wasn't happy either. 'Yes, c'mon, Roo. I've asked you not to do that already.'

'Sorry,' said Rueben, reluctantly moving the ramps out of the way.

'Alright,' said Mum. 'Pants on, Rueben. Shoes on, Oli. Noah, turn off the TV please.'

It was feeling like the normal before-school circus when Oli crouched down in front of Mum.

'Mum, I can't do up my laces,' he said.

Mum looked down at Oli from her wheelchair, his big eyes staring up at her. It was impossible for her to reach his shoes to help him. She forced a smile. 'Dad's double knots are better.'

Oli dashed over to Dad, who gave his son a hug before helping him tie his laces.

Mum picked up a knife, trying her best to cut the sandwiches on the wooden chopping board, but the board slipped, and the sandwiches fell onto the floor.

I knew she was angry at herself, at her situation. 'Mum, can we buy our own lunch today? It's Friday, remember?' I asked, looking to make a bad thing into a good one.

'Yes! Mum? Can we? Can we? Can I get a pie?' begged Rueben.

Oli liked to make his own decisions. 'Sausage roll!' he demanded.

Mum attempted to smile. 'Of course. It's Friday.' Her eyes glistened with tears, but she swallowed hard.

'Dad, come on, we're late,' whined Rueben.

Dad smiled sadly at Mum, quickly picking up the sandwiches from the floor and putting them in the bin. 'I'm sorry. We've gotta go. Please keep your phone next to you, okay?'

Oli and Rueben moved in to kiss Mum goodbye.

'Bye, Mum.'

'Bye, Mum.'

'Bye,' replied Mum. She looked up, waiting for a kiss from me, but I was already walking out the door.

'Bye, Mum.'

The door closed behind me. And Mum was left alone in the house, watching as the rest of us Blooms clambered into the car, Rueben bagsing the front seat like he did every day, using the same excuse. 'I'm older than Oli.'

'You're always older than me!' cried out Oli, outraged at the unfairness of it all.

I never cared about where in the car I sat, so it was always my brothers who were left fighting about it.

I could feel Mum's sad eyes on us as we reversed down the driveway.

CHAPTER 3

Back when I was four, a long time ago, Mum wore a cape to Halloween. Dad told us she was only a mum in the daytime. At night her true identity was a … superhero. Faster than lightning. Fighting evil. In-des-tructible. We believed him because with Mum, our life was an adventure.

Dad works as a photographer, but he's also always taking photos for the fun of it. One of his cameras is around his neck all the time, waiting for the perfect light, the perfect wave or the best facial expression. As a result, our home is full of photos. They hang on every available wall in every room of our house.

And they're mostly photos of us kids outdoors, surfing, playing, mucking around with Mum and Dad. Lots of photos of our life before Mum's accident.

There are also photos of Mum and Dad in all the places they travelled to before they had kids. There's one of Mum in somewhere exotic like Morocco, galloping a horse across a desert. But one of Dad's best photos, I reckon anyway, is a shot he took of Mum standing by the Barrenjoey Lighthouse. It takes pride of place on our sideboard. She looks strong and calm and ready to take on the world. Like a superhero.

We can see the lighthouse from our home. It's on the top of Barrenjoey Point above Palm Beach and there's a steep, sandy track that you can take that gets you right to the lighthouse. We used to go there all the time for picnics in summer, the five of us, racing each other to the top.

Mum said that after the accident it really hurt her to see that lighthouse. It was a reminder of all the things she could no longer do. So she'd pull the curtains in the living room shut, blocking out the view and the light and just sit in the dark, waiting for time to pass. Her mum, our Nana Jan, would come over during the day when we were at school, and find Mum sitting in a dark room. She'd do her best to cheer up Mum.

Pulling open the curtains, Nana Jan would say, 'You need some light and fresh air in here, love. Why don't you take a book out onto the lawn? Or do your exercises?'

Mum would silently watch her mother buzz around her, tidying the house, chatting about nothing much to fill the silence.

'Remember what that doctor in rehab said: you've got to keep your spirits up. What was his name? The nice Indian. Neil? Or maybe you could try one of those podcasts? I saw Bron at the supermarket. She says she can be hanging out the washing and solving a murder at the same time. Nihal! That's the doctor's name. I knew it sounded like Neil. I liked him. By the way, Bron was asking — when are you going to let her visit? Glass of wine with your girlfriends. Well overdue.'

Nana would continue to talk, and Mum was grateful for the help, but she was quietly wishing she could remain alone in the house with the curtains drawn shut.

*

Where we live in Sydney, on the Northern Beaches, we get some sick storms. The waves are enormous, great for surfing if you're feeling brave. They crash against the rocky headland, and the sky lights up with forked lightning. We had one of those massive storms around this time. The house shook, the enormous Norfolk pine trees that lined the beach swayed dangerously — nature was at its full force.

I love storms. But listening to the roaring thunder and pounding rain when you're tucked up in bed is one thing; it's not so great if you're a scruffy, little magpie chick who's fallen out of her nest in the dead of night.

I haven't forgotten that I told you this story was also about a magpie. And you've been wondering when she appears, right? Well, it's right about now ...

CHAPTER 4

The day after the big summer storm, the sun shone bright in a clear blue sky. Rueben, Oli and I woke early and ran down to the beach first thing, knowing we'd have the beach to ourselves. It was magic. We swam and mucked around for a while. Then we noticed all the driftwood and the broken branches that had fallen during the storm. We decided to put them to good use and began collecting the debris. After a couple of arguments around where we were going to build, we found the perfect location. A way back from the shoreline so the incoming tide wouldn't knock it over, and near to bushland so it would be protected from wind.

With the three of us working hard, it didn't take long until we had a proper hide-out with walls and a roof.

'I'll have my TV here and my couch here. Speakers over there,' said Oli, mapping out the space as he propped a branch against the side of the structure.

'It's a cool cubby house,' said Rueben, appreciating our good work.

I didn't quite agree with him though. 'It's not a cubby house,' I said. 'It's a fortress. Just for us. No grown-ups.'

That made it even better, and we all knew it. I imagined we would come down to our fortress every weekend, protecting its borders from outsiders and unwanted adults, where no-one could tell us what to do. Maybe we'd invite a couple of friends in, or maybe it would stay a fortress for the Blooms only.

I was thinking about all of this as we continued building, until I was distracted by a faint squeak from the nearby bushes.

'Did ya hear that?' I asked my brothers.

'Nah,' answered Rueben, who was probably also dreaming about plans for the fortress.

Oli was off grabbing another huge palm frond, humming to himself. He didn't even hear my question.

I stood still and listened again. There was another squeak. I went to investigate. As I crept closer to the noise, an Eastern Water Dragon, who'd been staring at me in stillness, startled and sprinted away. There was another little squeak. I crouched down and tried to find the source of the noise. After a few more seconds of rummaging around, I found it. In the undergrowth, at the base of a huge Norfolk pine, was a teeny tiny magpie chick. It looked terrified, and I realised the Eastern Water Dragon must have scared it. To something that small, the lizard would have looked like a carnivorous dinosaur. I glanced around to make sure there were no other chicks nearby. It was alone. There was no way I was going to just leave it there. If it had fallen from its nest high above, it was probably injured. I bundled it up as carefully as I could, called my brothers and took the chick home to Mum and Dad. The fortress was going to have to wait another day.

At home we found an old cane laundry basket and filled it with rags, and then gently placed the little chick on top. It continued to squeak and chatter.

Mum wasn't as pleased to meet the chick as I thought she would be. 'Maybe you should have left it there,' she said.

The chick huddled into itself, its damaged wing held out uncomfortably.

'It would've died out there alone, Mum,' I said, annoyed by her uncaring response. I focused on the chick. 'You hungry?' I tried to feed it a tiny piece of

bread that I'd soaked in water. 'Come on, little one.'
But it wouldn't eat. It just shivered. My brothers
were as concerned as I was.

'Maybe it doesn't like eating bread,' said Oli.

'We need worms,' suggested Rueben.

Dad came over from the kitchen with a bowl of
water and an eyedropper. 'Well, let's keep its fluids
up in the meantime.' He handed the bowl to me.
'Here, Snow, you do it.' Snow is my nickname.

I filled the dropper and tried to squeeze the water
into its beak, but most of it dripped out. The chick
continued to squeak. Was it a scared squeak or an
angry squeak? Or was it telling us it would rather
be sleeping and could we please just leave it alone?
We couldn't tell.

Mum shook her head. 'I think it'd be better off
at the vet.'

'Is it a boy or a girl?' asked Oli.

We all peered closely at the chick, having no idea
how to tell if it was a she or a he.

Rueben picked up Dad's phone and searched for magpie facts. 'Says here a magpie's gender can't be determined until after a year.'

'It's a girl,' I said confidently.

'How do you know that, Snow?' asked Dad.

I answered, 'I just do.'

The chick squeaked in a way that made her sound happy with my decision.

'See. She's agreeing with me,' I said with a giggle.

Dad said, 'Well, she needs a name. But maybe we keep it gender neutral just in case Noah's wrong.'

Mum grimaced. 'No, Cam. No names. We've got enough to worry about around here.' She wheeled herself out of the room, no longer willing to participate.

Despite Mum's lack of interest, I wasn't going to turn my back on the chick. I started thinking of names for her. It didn't take me long to come up with the perfect choice. 'Penguin,' I said to Dad and my brothers.

'Why Penguin?' asked Dad.

''Cos she's black and white.'

'What about Zebra then?' suggested Rueben.

'Or Skunk?' added Dad.

Oli piped up. 'Or Panda?'

'Panda's good,' said Dad.

'Magician's Wand? Soccer Ball?' Oli was on a roll.

'Or Chess Board?' said Rueben, which had to be the craziest suggestion of them all. But that's Rueben for you.

Even the baby chick disagreed with Rueben. She puffed out her chest and stretched her good wing. I knew what that meant.

'Penguin. Her name is Penguin,' I said firmly, and that was the end of the discussion.

CHAPTER 5

The first night that Penguin stayed in our house, I couldn't sleep. I was worried about her. Who knows what she was thinking? She was probably missing her mum and dad. Maybe she was even having nightmares about that Eastern Water Dragon? I crept down to the living room with a torch and was relieved to see her still in the laundry basket. I think I scared her a bit when I accidentally shone the torch right in her eyes. She squeaked and I decided she'd be much happier sleeping in my room with me. So I carefully carried the laundry basket back to my room, placed it down beside the bed, gave her feathers a little stroke and hopped back into bed. It was the right decision. We both slept better after that.

*

Because I was the one who'd found her, I was in charge of looking after Penguin and finding food for her. I'd get up before anyone else was awake, run out into the garden and dig for worms. And because it was early and quiet, and I was alone, I'd think about Mum and her accident. It was like Mum had been stolen from us. She used to surf with us, skate with us, play soccer in the sand with us. She was awesome. We didn't talk about it at all, but I think we all felt the same sadness.

Luckily for us, once Penguin arrived, she became a cheeky, fluffy distraction, and slowly but surely we all felt a little bit less sad. It turned out she seemed to really like being part of a human family. My brothers and I would hang out on our rooftop,

Penguin perched on my hand, while Oli and Rueben were skating.

'Look at this. Penguin! Look!' Oli would yell as he skated past.

Penguin would watch them, wide-eyed. She seemed to think a human boy on wheels was super exciting. Sometimes the excitement got too much for her.

'Euugh. Wait ... Did she just poo on you?' asked Rueben, watching the white liquid run down my hand.

Oli giggled. 'She needs a nappy.'

'No, you do,' said Rueben.

'No, you do,' said Oli. 'For your farts.'

I didn't mind about the poo. She was a bird. It was bird poo. No big deal.

'Hey, Penguin! This is how you fly!' said Rueben as he ran to the edge of the roof and jumped off, landing on the trampoline below. He bounced back up, with his arms in the air ... 'I'm flying!' he yelled.

Oli laughed, enjoying Roo's bravery.

'You try it, you chicken,' Rueben taunted Oli, who giggled some more as Rueben pretended to fly like a bird, but Oli stayed where he was on the roof.

Penguin and I didn't like Rueben showing off like that. 'Ignore him, Peng.' Penguin had a long way to go before she was ready to fly. She didn't need to rush.

Our new family member's arrival coincided with more changes in the Bloom household. To make sure Mum could move around freely in her wheelchair, Dad decided he was going to renovate. So one of our doorways was going to be widened. And that meant Dad with a sledgehammer. Which was really messy ... and loud.

Penguin and I didn't mind though. We would still hang out in the living room, in the middle of the demolition, despite the noise.

'It's yummy, see? Come on, Peng. You gotta eat.'

I'd found some juicy earthworms, which must have looked delicious to a hungry bird. Penguin was curious and chattering away. She finally gave one of the worms a peck.

'Dad, look. Almost.'

Dad stopped his work to see Penguin pecking at the worm before she jumped down from my lap and decided to go for a walk. 'Nice work, Snow. It's a start.'

I'd been doing some research. 'Google says birds learn to sing in their sleep. They dream of their mother's song.'

At that moment Mum entered the room in her wheelchair.

Dad smiled. 'No kidding. Bit like you, Sam. You used to sing to the kids when they were little. What was the —'

'Mum, stop!' I shouted.

Mum froze in panic, breathing hard.

I ran over to Penguin, who was right in front of Mum's wheel. 'You almost ran over her,' I said, angry at Mum.

Mum got angry back. 'It shouldn't be here, Snow. It needs to go to a vet, where it can be looked after properly.'

'But I'm looking after her.'

'Yeah? And who's gonna clean up its mess? Me?'

'I will! I never asked you to!' I said, really angry now. I was taking responsibility for Penguin. Why couldn't she see that?

Dad intervened. 'Hey! Don't yell at your mum, mate.'

Mum and I were still fuming when Nana Jan sailed through the door.

'Cooee. Only me!' she called out cheerily as she walked down the hallway. 'I can't stay. Just dropping back the sheets.'

Dad smiled tensely. 'Thanks, Jan. We do have a laundry. We can wash the sheets ourselves ...'

Nana gave me a big hug, but was shocked to see a chick in the house. 'Snow. What … is … that?'

I explained. 'Her name's Penguin. She's a baby magpie. She fell out of her nest.'

Nana moved closer, putting on her glasses to get a better look.

Penguin chattered to Nana as she tried to flap her broken wing.

'Don't like the look of that wing.' Nana frowned. 'Poor little mite.'

I reassured Nana. 'She'll be okay.'

I picked up Penguin and left the room, but heard Mum say to Nana, 'Don't look at me like that. I've tried to tell him. And Cam.'

Nana answered, 'That bird looks like it could die any minute. And what's gonna happen if they get attached to it, hm?'

I didn't wait to hear any more of that conversation.

So, as you can see, in those first days after Penguin arrived, we were still adjusting to our new situation, and not every family member was pro-Penguin. But she needed my help, and I was going to look after her, no matter what. I just had to convince Mum and Dad to let me keep her until she could look after herself.

CHAPTER 6

After only a few days with us Blooms, Penguin felt like one of the gang. On the last day of the school holidays, we were in the living room, just hanging out.

Oli wasn't always super sensitive about Mum's condition. But he was only little, so nobody blamed him. He poked Mum's leg and asked, 'Can you feel this?'

Mum shook her head.

Oli poked her leg a bit further down. 'Can you feel this?'

Mum shook her head no again.

Oli called it a superpower, but Mum didn't see it that way.

I think Penguin could sense Mum's unhappiness and did her best to cheer her up. She cheep-cheeped at her, expecting some kind of response.

'Mum, Penguin's talking to you,' I prompted.

Mum just stared off into space, in her own world. 'What?'

'Why don't you like her?' I asked.

Mum shrugged. 'It's a wild bird, Noah, which means it can't stay here forever, right?'

I'd made a special breakfast mix for Penguin, but she was still not great at taking food from me. 'C'mon, Peng,' I coaxed. 'You've gotta get your strength up.'

Rueben was as helpful as ever. 'She obviously doesn't like it, Noah.'

'She should,' I said. 'I made it just like they said online, with bugs and eggs and stuff.'

Rueben stuck out his tongue. 'You try it, see whether it tastes good.'

'Shut up, Rueben.'

Mum just sighed. Normally I'd get in trouble for telling my brother to shut up.

Dad arrived back from a job, and his presence made everyone relax slightly.

'Hey? Sorry I'm late. I was s'posed to be taking a normal family portrait, but turns out they all hate each other's guts. And mine too apparently. So that was a bit of fun.'

He dumped his photographic equipment on the bench, and then went over to kiss Mum. 'Hey, how are you? How's the pain: one to ten?'

Mum looked angry at him for asking, but said, 'I'm fine.'

Dad turned to Penguin. 'And you? G'day, gorgeous.'

He tickled the top of Penguin's head, and she sneezed.

'*Gesundheit*,' said Dad.

Everyone laughed except for Mum.

'I thought we'd get fish and chips for dinner?' suggested Dad with a grin. 'Eat on the beach?'

'Ye-es!' said Rueben and Oli.

'Can I bring Penguin?' I asked.

'Sure,' said Dad. 'And Sam, I could carry you —'

Mum grimaced. 'No.'

Dad persevered. 'It's beautiful down there. Come on. The boys can jump in for a dip.'

'Please, Mum?' begged Rueben.

'I don't think so. You boys go. I'm almost ready for bed anyway.' Mum wouldn't budge.

Dad tried again. 'It's too early for bed, Sam ...'

But Mum began to wheel herself away.

'Please, Mum?' asked Oli in his sweetest voice.

Mum turned to Oli, trying to hold back tears. 'Sorry, bub, just a bit tired.' She gave him a big hug. 'Bring me back a shell, okay?'

Oli nodded, feeling a little better. He liked having a mission.

Mum left and headed for her bedroom.

Dad turned to us. 'Grab your towels while I help Mum, okay?'

While we gathered our beach stuff, I overheard Mum and Dad talking. He was helping her get ready for bed.

'Never ask me that question in front of the boys again,' Mum said angrily to Dad.

'What question?' he asked, confused as to why she was so upset.

'How am I. I don't want to have to lie to them, Cam. Do you understand?'

Dad sighed. 'Okay. I'm sorry.'

Roo and Oli were calling him, ready to leave by that stage, so he kissed Mum goodbye and left her alone.

Down at the beach, Penguin played on the sand with me and watched seagulls fly overhead. I reckon she missed her mum, just like I did. I found a really nice shell that I gave to Oli to give to Mum when he got back home. I knew she'd like it. Then we ate fish and chips and oysters on the headland, looking out over the sea. Dad seemed particularly sad — I knew he was worried about Mum, and he missed her being with us too.

There should be nothing else to mention about that day, but unfortunately that was not the end of it. We were woken in the middle of the night, with a sickly-sounding Rueben calling out to Dad.

Turns out the oysters gave both my brothers bad food poisoning. There was a lot of gross vomiting, and Dad was slipping around the bathroom floor, cleaning up the mess that happens when there are two kids vomiting and only one toilet bowl to vomit in. Luckily for Penguin and me, we didn't like oysters, so we could stay well clear of the bathroom.

When Oli and Rueben had finally stopped, and Dad returned them to their beds, I heard him trudge wearily back into his bedroom. Mum was crying. I knew she had wanted to help, to comfort Oli and Rueben. She had always been there to look after us when anything went wrong. And now she couldn't run to us when we called to her.

I did some internet research. Twenty million people holiday in Thailand every year. That's a lot of people, right? And more importantly, there are twenty million *other* people that this could have happened to. There are forty million other hands that could have touched the railing that Mum leant on before she fell. A railing that was fifteen years old. That means there was a total of 5,475 other days in its lifetime that it could have broken.

But it waited for Mum.

And I ... I haven't really mentioned this before now, because, well, I'm the one that had noticed the platform, and I'm the one that told her to come up and take a look at it with me. If I hadn't pointed it out, if I hadn't ...

Anyway, I needed to give Penguin an extra-big hug before I fell back asleep that night.

CHAPTER 7

A new term began, and Oli, Rueben and I had to go back to school. Dad was busy with work and I was really worried about Penguin being lonely without us all there. So I needed back-up.

While the others were piling into the car, ready to get driven to school, I went to Mum's bedroom and knocked on the door. She hadn't got up to help with our school lunches, so I knew she probably wasn't feeling too good.

'Mum?' I called out quietly.

There was no answer.

'Mum?' I said again.

'Come in, Snow,' said Mum, sounding tired.

I came in. She was lying in bed, staring at the ceiling. 'Can you look after Penguin for me today, Mum? She's not eating very well.'

Mum didn't answer for a long while.

'Mum?'

'Yeah, okay, Noah.'

Dad was calling me to hurry up by that stage, so all I had time to do was give Peng a quick pat before sprinting to the car. I spent all day worrying about her too. Couldn't concentrate on schoolwork or what my friends had done on the holidays or anything normal.

But Mum told me later what that first day alone had been like for her and Penguin. Two minutes after the car had driven down the driveway, Mum heard Penguin start to cheep. And she got louder and louder and didn't stop. She was obviously wondering where my brothers and I had gone. She was used to being entertained by us.

Mum just wanted to stay in bed, but Penguin's cheeping was driving her crazy, so she managed to get herself out of bed and into her wheelchair. She was angry by this stage. She wheeled herself out to the living room and there was Penguin in her laundry basket, cheep-cheeping away like a baby bird wanting her mother to feed her.

Mum felt a bit sorry for her and offered her some of the food I'd left for her. But the cheeky bird wouldn't even take it. Mum got even more annoyed and decided to turn on some music to block out the sound of Penguin's cheeping. Now that she'd been forced to get up, Mum went to the bathroom to brush her teeth. By the time she came back from the bathroom, Penguin was no longer in the laundry basket. Mum couldn't see Penguin and couldn't hear Penguin. Where had she gone?

Mum turned off the music, and a game of cat and mouse began. (A game of Mum and bird doesn't sound quite right — so you'll have to be okay with cat and mouse.) Mum wheeled herself carefully around the room, but now Penguin had gone into stealth mode and stopped cheeping.

Then, out of nowhere, Oli's remote-controlled truck drove under Mum's wheelchair. Penguin had clearly stepped on the remote control and caused it to move. Clever bird!

Mum wasn't impressed though. She carried on looking around the living room for the escapee and didn't see Penguin sneak off into my bedroom. It wasn't tidy, and I can imagine Penguin running around, playing with my underwear and all the toys I had around the place. She hid under the bed, and eventually Mum found her there, pecking away at an old favourite toy, a knitted monkey called Mr Murphy that I'd been given by a family friend when I was really small.

Mum wasn't going to let Penguin just hang out under my bed for the rest of the day, and she told me she grabbed a hockey stick to try to get Penguin out.

It wasn't easy, but Mum eventually scooped Penguin out from under the bed like a hockey puck, and Penguin raced down the hallway and out of sight.

Well, luckily Mum is always up for a challenge, and Penguin was certainly being challenging, so Mum continued her hunt for the baby magpie. There was a crash from the living room, where a couple of small clay vases had mysteriously fallen off the shelf. But there was no sign of Penguin.

Finally Mum heard chirping from the outside laundry, where we store jars and jars of honey from the beehives up on the roof. She wheeled herself out there and found Penguin stuck in a tray of honey, feathers sticky and dripping, looking scared and panicky. Game over. Mum: one. Bird: zero.

Mum gently picked up Penguin and took her back to the kitchen, where she washed her down and even blow-dried her feathers, as though Penguin was a customer at a hair salon. Mum said the little bird cooed contently the whole time.

When Mum had finished with the grooming session and was absent-mindedly stroking her, Penguin looked up at Mum. And just stared at her. Mum stared back. She said Penguin made her smile. And it felt like the first time she'd smiled in a long while.

I'd told Mum how special Penguin was, but she hadn't seen it until just then. And I reckon Penguin and Mum decided to become friends from that point on.

That night at dinner, Mum seemed more relaxed. Her friend Bron had dropped around a lasagne, and it was delicious. Penguin was hanging around Mum's feet, keeping a close eye on her newest buddy. I noticed, but didn't say anything, just in case it broke the spell. I had no problem sharing Penguin with Mum, especially if it meant Mum might become a little bit less sad.

While Oli was telling us about school, Penguin started dragging something out of my bedroom.

I got up and saw it was Mr Murphy, my old knitted monkey. It was clear Mum wasn't the only friend Penguin had made today. I put Mr Murphy into Penguin's laundry basket, and Penguin pecked Mr Murphy happily. Oli and Rueben decided Penguin had fallen in love.

'Penguin and Mr Murphy sitting in a tree. K-I-S-S-I-N-G,' they sang, laughing.

Mum and Dad were smiling at Penguin's antics too. It felt good. It was like we were reminded of how we used to be all the time, before Mum's accident.

And I knew I needed to make the most of it.

'Can Penguin stay?' I asked Mum and Dad. But really it was only a question for Mum.

Dad looked over at Mum, and she nodded slowly. 'Only until she's strong enough, Noah, okay? She's not meant to be stuck inside.'

That was good enough for me!

CHAPTER 8

Penguin got stronger and fatter as the days went by, but she couldn't seem to use her wings to fly. That didn't stop her from becoming a very busy member of the Bloom family. She was never far away from us. She'd go biking with us, snooze on the sofa with us, take a sticky beak (literally) when we were harvesting our honey.

And she kept close to Mum. They spent a lot of time together. Penguin would sing to Mum, and Mum would talk to Penguin about things. I think she told Penguin things she wasn't able to talk to us about. And because Penguin was such a good listener, Mum felt better getting the words and thoughts out of her head. There was no judgement. And Penguin was in a similar situation, I guess. She was a bird that was meant to fly. But she couldn't. They really understood each other.

There were good days and bad days, and I knew Penguin made every day a little bit better for us Blooms. Especially the bad ones.

A few weeks after Penguin had become an official family member, she got to meet Aunty Kylie, Mum's sister, who had just come back from a yoga retreat overseas.

Dad and I were on the roof, smoking the beehives, so we were doing our best astronaut impression, dressed in our beekeeping suits.

Oli and Rueben were messing around on the trampoline.

'Aunty Kylie's back!' yelled out Oli as her car pulled into the driveway.

Aunty Kylie got out of the car and went over to the trampoline. Oli launched into her arms. 'Hey, scamp! Hey, Roo,' she said. Rueben kept jumping on the trampoline.

I came to the edge of the roof and waved.

Dad wandered over and puffed the bee smoker. 'G'day, stranger.'

Aunty Kylie smiled and waved to us before heading into the house to find Mum. I ran in after her and went to my bedroom to take off the beekeeping suit. It got really hot in that thing.

'Sammy?' called out Aunty Kylie.

Mum came down the hallway to meet her. They hugged.

'Still in the chair then?' said Aunty Kylie, joking.

'You look good,' said Mum, ignoring the joke.

'Yeah, it was pretty amazing. Didn't speak for twenty-one days. Or drink.'

Mum smiled. 'Think we should get Mum to go?'

The two sisters laughed as Nana Jan entered, placing some groceries on the table.

'How about I put the coffee on? Do you need anything, darling?' Nana sorted through the groceries, keeping an eye on her daughters.

'I'm fine, Mum,' answered Mum.

Aunty Kylie had obviously come with a purpose. 'So! I would kill for a glass of wine. When was the last time you went out, Sam?'

Mum got defensive. 'I go out.'

'Where? I don't mean to the doctor's. I mean really out.'

Mum shrugged.

'Come on. What do you think? Let's go out for lunch.'

'Would do us all the world of good,' said Nana, nodding enthusiastically.

I came over to Aunty Kylie and placed Penguin on her arm. They had not been officially introduced. 'This is Penguin.'

'Oh yes, that's right, I heard all about you,' Aunty Kylie said to the magpie.

Penguin puffed up her feathers proudly. She assumed the gossip was all complimentary.

'So you're a crazy bird person now,' Aunty Kylie said with a cheeky grin, looking at Mum. 'Could be worse, I suppose.'

Nana couldn't help muttering under her breath, 'Could it?'

It was clear Nana had not yet warmed to our beautiful Penguin.

And Penguin could tell when she was being dissed. She flapped her wings in outrage, and Aunty Kylie squealed in surprise. It made Mum laugh out loud.

*

Nana Jan and Aunty Kylie convinced Mum to go out to lunch, and it turned out not to do Mum the world of good at all. Mum saw everyone going about their lives like normal down at the beach, and it made her feel awful. She bumped into her closest friend, Bron, who was nursing and doing all the school-mum stuff, and it just made Mum angry that she didn't have that life anymore. She didn't tell Nana Jan or Aunty Kylie how she was feeling. She just held it all inside until they'd dropped her back home.

We came in from the beach with Dad to find the living room covered in broken glass from the photo frames, and photos strewn everywhere. Mum was sitting in the middle of the room, not making eye contact with any of us. Dad told us to jump in the shower so he could have a talk with Mum. We'd never been so obedient. We all pretty much ran from the room.

But I overheard their conversation.

When she'd got home, Mum waited until she was by herself ... and had a total temper tantrum.

Penguin watched her, squawking at her to calm down, but Mum didn't listen. She smashed all the photos on the living room wall with a broom. Photos of her life before her accident. When she could walk, run, surf, work and play with her kids. She was so angry that she'd lost the life she'd loved.

Dad was sad rather than angry when he saw what she'd done. 'All those things we did, and the kids, and all our trips.'

'I know,' said Mum.

'Those photos. They're us, Sam. They're who we are.'

Mum sighed. 'Then I'll put them back up.'

'I'm not saying that, Sam,' said Dad. 'I'm just saying, if you'd told me that's how you felt, or — or ...'

He stopped talking.

Mum looked at Dad frowning at the bare wall, not speaking.

'Cam, please stop staring at the wall,' she said.

'Yeah, no, I get it,' said Dad after a pause.

Mum was wary. 'Get what?'

'That you want to … erase yourself. Who you were.' He turned to her. 'But you're still you, Sam.'

Mum shook her head. 'No, I'm not. That's the point. I'm —'

'You are. You're still my wife. You're still the boys' mother.'

Mum got angry again. 'No, I'm not, Cam. That's someone else.' She put her hand to her chest. 'This is not me. Not my body. Not my life. I can't look at her,' she said, directing her gaze at the photo of her near the lighthouse, '… at that.'

Not wanting to argue, Dad started picking up glass shards.

Mum was crying now. 'Look at me!'

Dad didn't look at her. He kept looking at the photo of her and the lighthouse. He ended up sweeping up the mess and making us dinner. But he was unusually quiet. We all were. After dinner,

Dad decided to have a surf by himself. Mum went to bed and Penguin stayed with her, keeping her company.

And I watched old videos on my laptop of Mum and me climbing up to the Barrenjoey Lighthouse.

It was definitely one of our 'bad' days.

CHAPTER 9

As Penguin got more confident, she wanted to spend more time in the garden. Mum would find her strutting along the windowsill, backlit by the first rays of the morning sun, listening to birdsong, impatient to get outdoors.

Mum would open the door and Penguin would trot happily outside.

We have a big frangipani tree in our front yard. And I could imagine, from Penguin's point of view, that tree was gigantic, like some magical beanstalk reaching up to the sky, full of twisting branches, huge leaves, sweet flowers and insects crawling over it.

Mum realised perhaps Penguin was ready to try out sitting in a tree. As a housebound bird, this tree was exotic and otherworldly. Mum picked up Penguin and reached out towards the tree, putting her on a low branch.

'Birds love this tree,' she said, coaxing Penguin on.

Penguin was a bit worried, but there was so much to explore from this high off the ground. She spotted a trail of insects following an unseen highway into the branches above. This was an unexpected snack and she pecked a few of them happily, getting braver the further up she went.

Mum watched Penguin discovering a new world and she relaxed a bit herself. It was a beautiful morning and she could hear magpies singing.

Penguin listened to the magpies too. The singing came from a tree a few houses away. Mum and Penguin both watched a majestic bird flying towards the sound of the singing, homing in on its mate. Penguin looked at the bird flying and decided to give it a shot. She opened her wings.

Mum got excited for her. 'C'mon, Peng. Give it a go.'

Encouraged, Penguin began to flap her wings. Mum held her breath. Penguin took a jump and ... PLOP! She hit the ground. Disappointed but not hurt. She cheeped up at Mum ruefully, grooming her ruffled feathers.

'Don't worry, Peng. Next time.'

Dad was strolling around the garden taking photos, and he took a photo of Mum enjoying the sunshine.

He walked up to her. 'Maybe we should try something different,' he said with a grin, pulling a pamphlet out of his back pocket.

Mum was a bit suspicious. 'What do you mean?'

Dad passed Mum the ad he'd been carrying around for a few days, waiting for the right time to mention it to her. It was an advertisement for kayaking lessons.

Mum took a quick glance at it. 'Are you serious?' she asked with a frown.

'Come on, Sam, you love the water,' encouraged Dad.

'You don't get it,' said Mum, shaking her head in disbelief. She started to wheel herself back into the house. 'What happens when I fall in? This is for you, not for me.'

Dad wasn't about to give up. He was desperately wanting things to get better and he thought that kayaking could give Mum something to look forward to. He followed her into the house.

Rueben, Oli and I were in Rueben's room, playing video games, but we could all hear their 'conversation' getting louder. It was about to turn into another argument.

'What are you scared of?' asked Dad. 'That you'll drown? Because —'

'Dying is the one thing I'm not scared of,' Mum replied.

'The worst that can happen is you'll feel embarrassed. But unless you try —'

Mum yelled now. 'Every moment of my life is embarrassing! I don't need something else that makes me feel useless, Cam!'

'So what do you need? Because I'm running out of ideas. The boys and I, we're struggling!' yelled back Dad.

'Oh, *you're* struggling?'

'Yes, it's all of us, Sam!'

'No, it's not,' Mum answered stubbornly.

At this point in the argument Rueben decided he didn't want to hear anymore, and he climbed out of the window with Oli and headed up to the roof.

Dad's voice got a little softer. 'Just tell me what you want.'

So did Mum's. 'I want to walk my kids to school. I want to go to the beach, get dressed without your help. I want a day without pain. That's what I want. Anything but this.' Mum wheeled herself into her bedroom and slammed the door behind her.

Rueben stuck his head back in his bedroom window. 'Noah, you coming up for a skate?'

'Nah. I'm gonna go check on Dad.'

Rueben nodded and disappeared again.

Penguin was with me and we both walked into the kitchen. Dad was looking really sad. I wanted to say something, but I wasn't sure what he needed to hear.

Dad sighed, and then put his hand in some bird poo that Penguin had left behind on the bench. Instead of joking about it like he normally did, Dad yelled at me. 'Will you please clean up this mess!'

He strode outside angrily, ignoring Penguin, who was warbling at him sympathetically. Maybe there just wasn't anything either of us could say that would make Dad's pain any better.

But I could clean up the bird poo. That was

something. I grabbed a cloth and wiped up the mess. Penguin was behaving weirdly as I washed down the bench. She seemed jumpy and was making a lot of noise.

I told her to keep quiet, but she wasn't interested in what I had to say. Her squawking got louder as she walked towards Mum's closed bedroom door. I realised that Peng wanted to check in on Mum.

When I opened the door, Mum was lying on the floor, her face twisted in pain. She'd fallen out of her wheelchair and hadn't been able to get back up.

Penguin scuttled in and went to Mum's side.

'Mum? Can I help?' I asked, rushing in to her.

'Okay. Thanks, bud. Just lost my balance,' she replied.

'I'll get Dad,' I said.

'No,' said Mum firmly. 'Just give me a hand, Snow.'

I carefully tried to lift Mum onto the bed, but I wasn't strong enough. She tried to lift herself, and I pulled as hard as I could. Penguin hopped up onto the bed, wanting to help, but she was as useless as I was.

I was frustrated. 'Dad!' I yelled out, panicked, hoping he could hear me.

'No. It's okay. I'm fine,' said Mum. 'Grab me a pillow.'

I passed her a pillow. Mum sat uncomfortably on the floor, breathing heavily, still in pain.

'Mum?'

'It's okay, Snow. Just let me catch my breath for a bit.'

I tried to be helpful like Dad. 'How much is it hurting, Mum? One to ten?'

But Mum didn't want me to see her like this. 'You go for a surf, Noah. Dad'll be in soon.'

I wasn't going to leave her like this. 'That's okay. I can stay,' I replied.

But she put on her stern Mum voice. 'Just go, Noah! Please.'

She lay down on the floor, the pillow under her head.

I left the room, but I felt terrible. I'd let both Dad and Mum down. I was there and I hadn't made either of them feel better. Penguin stayed with Mum and I went back to my room. I had a lump in my throat the size of a small car, but I didn't cry. I just sat there, staring out the window.

I think that was the time we all felt our most hopeless. Rueben and Oli were on the roof, trying to pretend they hadn't heard Mum and Dad fight; Dad was furious and had stormed off down the road; Mum was in pain and angry with everyone; and I felt useless and really, really sad. We were sinking and we didn't know how to get ourselves out of the quicksand.

But remember, there was one more member of the family. And us Blooms needed her now more than ever. And boy, did she rise to the occasion.

CHAPTER 10

While I sat on my bed feeling miserable, Mum was lying on her bedroom floor, sobbing with anger and frustration. Penguin looked down at her from her position on the bed, realising she needed to do something. She stared at Mum, her bright black eyes full of determination. Mum stared back, a little confused by Penguin's mood change.

Penguin slowly started flapping her wings with strong, confident beats.

Mum frowned. What was going on?

Then Penguin took a few running steps towards the end of the bed and took off.

Mum gasped.

Penguin's wings stretched wide. She started to fly, FLY around the room. Awkwardly at first, but then she did a couple of loops of the bedroom before swooping out the door and down the hallway.

Mum stopped crying and shouted, 'Penguin! Boys!'

I ran out of my bedroom to see Penguin FLY down the hallway and out the front door.

'Peng!' I yelled in amazement and ran out the front door after her. Rueben and Oli were still on the roof, and they could see Penguin flying low around the garden. They were shouting encouragement to her.

'C'mon, Peng! You can do it, Penguin!'

Penguin soared over our backyard, a little wobbly at first but then she steadied. She circled above the trampoline, then gained height and flew over the roof, past the beehives, with Rueben and Oli cheering her on.

Penguin felt the wind on her face and the power of her wings. She heard the sounds of birds all around her with a clarity she'd never experienced before. She could sense the patterns in the wind.

Dad came up the driveway, running, hearing his boys yelling, and it took him a minute to realise it was joyous yelling. And then he looked up. 'Oh my gosh. Is that you, Penguin?'

Oli, Rueben and I were ecstatic, watching Penguin swoop and climb like a professional.

Dad ran into Mum's bedroom, where she could hear the whoops of laughter, and she was now crying with happiness. 'Penguin's flying?' she asked Dad.

He scooped her up and placed her in the wheelchair. 'There's no way you're missing this, Sam,' he said, and the two of them sped out into the yard.

I pointed to where Penguin was flying and we all just watched her having what was absolutely the best day of her life. She swooped and circled, and we were all shouting encouragement.

Mum sat in her chair, her heart bursting with pride. Penguin was such a clever and determined bird.

Eventually Penguin flew back into our yard and landed in Mum's lap, a little clumsily. In fact, she fell flat on her face. She was probably exhausted. But she wanted to share her success with us. She scrambled to a standing position and looked up at her adopted family.

'That was amazing!' shouted Oli from the roof.

Rueben added, 'Nice job, Peng.'

I gave her a celebratory pat. 'Yes! Told you you'd fly one day, Peng.'

Mum cradled Penguin's tiny head and gave her a kiss. It felt awesome for us all to share this special moment with her. And that wasn't the only bonus.

Seeing Penguin do something she thought might be impossible gave Mum the lift she'd been needing. Later that night, Mum found the kayaking brochure Dad had given her on the kitchen table. She picked it up and glanced at it again, this time with an open mind. She took a deep breath in and a deep breath out. Mum knew she wouldn't be able to walk again, but perhaps it was time to return to the water ...

CHAPTER 11

As you can imagine, Dad was thrilled when Mum told him she was willing to give kayaking a go, so it didn't take long before lessons had been organised. We all accompanied a really nervous Mum to her first session at Narrabeen Lakes, about a half-hour drive from home.

It was there that we met Gaye for the first time. She was this terrific larger-than-life Kiwi lady who was going to play a really important part in Mum's life from this point forward. With a no-nonsense type of attitude, Gaye joked, had a wicked laugh and didn't take no for an answer. We weren't sure it was going to work out when we first met her, because she was a bit, ah, I guess you'd say, a bit 'in your face'.

She waved to us from the shoreline of the lake. Oh, and she was loud. 'Hellooo! You must be the Blooms. I'm Gaye.'

She robustly shook hands with Mum and Dad.

'I'm Cameron. Hi. We spoke on the phone,' said Dad, sounding a little nervous himself.

Gaye looked at Mum. 'Cameron tells me you're quite the surfer.'

Mum shrugged. 'Was.'

Gaye continued. 'And a nurse. And a mum. By the look of these jokers,' she pointed to us boys, 'it can't be a walk in the park.'

We all laughed.

'You seem a bit nervous, Sam,' Gaye said.

'Well, I'm in a wheelchair,' answered Mum with a high-pitched laugh.

Gaye gave her a wide smile. 'I can see that. Wouldn't you rather be in a kayak?'

Mum smiled. I could tell she was wondering if it was too late to cancel the whole thing and head back home, but she slowly nodded in agreement, and Gaye didn't waste another minute. She and Dad carried Mum down to the water's edge and placed her carefully in the kayak. My brothers and I stayed close by, watching.

'Hold the back, Cameron, and I'll get the front,' instructed Gaye. They dragged the kayak fully into the water, and Mum wobbled a bit. Dad entered the shallow water to help steady the kayak.

'Pass the paddle to Sam please, Cameron,' said Gaye, moving back a few steps. 'Right, I want you to practise paddling,' she said to Mum.

Dad was holding the front of the kayak, looking on edge.

'Gentle hands, Cameron.' Gaye smiled at Mum. 'Gee, he goes in strong, doesn't he? Think of it like you're swimming, Sam, but you're gonna scoop the water back with your paddle instead of your hand. Feel it on your blade so you get a good catch.'

Mum began to paddle slowly, though Dad still held the kayak so she wasn't moving.

Gaye nodded. 'Eyes straight ahead. If you look to your side, you'll lean to the side.'

Mum concentrated hard, and soon she graduated to paddling the kayak alone in the shallow water. Dad got out and sat with us to watch her progress. The stress had left his body now.

Gaye stayed close to Mum, walking beside her as she paddled. 'The more comfortable you feel, the quicker you can go.'

Dad couldn't help himself — he started snapping photos of Mum on the lake. I didn't blame him. It was pretty sick to see her out there, gliding through the water.

Gaye continued to give Mum instruction. 'Relax and breathe. Looking a bit tense there, Sam.'

It was true. Mum had this massive frown on her face, she was concentrating so hard.

After a few moments more, Gaye dragged the kayak into deeper water. 'Okay, okay. Now we've come to the most important part of the lesson. I want you to tip over.'

'What?' said Mum, alarmed, thinking she was just getting the hang of the paddling bit and could calm down a little.

'You heard me. Get in there,' replied Gaye with a smile.

Mum laughed, hoping it was a joke. 'No way.'

'Come on. What's the worst thing that can happen?'

'I could drown,' said Mum honestly.

Gaye wasn't worried. 'Pfft! You can swim, can't you?'

Mum shrugged. 'I could before the accident.'

'Well, you still have your arms. They've gotta be good for something. Come on. It's like riding a bike.'

'Yeah. And I can't do that either.'

Gaye stepped it up a notch. 'Don't make me tip you out, Sam.'

'You wouldn't.'

'Oh, I tip people all the time. I'm known for it,' challenged Gaye, a twinkle in her eye.

At that point Mum looked over to us. I could practically read her thoughts: *We chose the wrong kayaking teacher. This woman is a crazed lunatic. Get me out of the water and away from her now!*

But she said nothing. And we looked back at her, trying to help her be brave.

Gaye stayed at the tip of the kayak, watching Mum. Mum began tentatively to lean to one side … but stopped.

'I can't. I can't do it.'

'This is the easy part,' said Gaye. 'This is *falling* off the bike.'

Mum's anger rose to the surface in an instant. 'I SAID I CAN'T!' she growled at Gaye.

I turned to Dad, really worried for Mum. 'She doesn't have to, does she?'

Dad remained calm. He said quietly, 'Wait. Watch.'

Gaye did not back down. She stayed right there, waiting for Mum to be ready, nodding to her with silent encouragement.

Finally Mum took a deep breath and started to lean. And this time she kept leaning until she fell into the water with a big splash.

I think we all held our breath, waiting for her to reappear, but it didn't take long. She broke the surface with a gasp of air, her arms keeping her afloat. She floated on her back, looking up at the sky.

Gaye let her enjoy the moment, the weightlessness of floating. It was clear that Gaye was not a crazed lunatic. In fact, she was exactly the coach Mum needed. A strong, supportive and stubborn teacher.

We were back on the shore, shouting and cheering, Dad taking more photos. In a matter of days, we had found out that Penguin could fly and Mum could swim.

CHAPTER 12

As soon as we got home from Narrabeen Lakes, I had to tell Penguin what had happened with Mum. It was a big deal and I knew our youngest family member would be proud of her. Mum was rinsing off under the outdoor shower and Penguin flew over to be with her, chirping and warbling contently, singing Mum's praises as the water splashed her feathers.

Later that evening, after us boys had gone to bed, Mum and Dad lit the fire pit and sat looking out at the view of the beach, talking like they used to before the accident. (This is one of the things that I didn't know at the time, but Dad told me about later.)

Penguin, of course, was close by. Dad put her on the frangipani tree. 'It'll soon be time for you to move out of home, girl,' he said to her. 'Or start paying rent.'

He walked back and sat next to Mum, who was watching the bright red glowing coals in the pit.

'You think she's okay out there?' asked Mum.

'She's ten feet away, Sam. I think she'll survive,' said Dad with a grin.

Mum nodded, not ready to give up her friend just yet.

Dad looked at Mum proudly. 'You were incredible today. Gaye thinks you've got talent.'

Mum laughed. 'At least I made the kids smile. Thanks for pushing me. I'm sorry you have to live with this.'

Dad shook his head vehemently. 'Are you kidding? I consider myself the luckiest man alive.'

'Oh, shut up. How can you say that?' Mum asked him.

Dad got serious. 'Because for a night I sat thinking I'd never see you again. But I did. And I do. Every day.'

Mum kissed his hand.

Dad continued. 'So I've been reading up on magpies. Turns out they mate for life.'

'Really?'

'Totally. One and only soulmate. They find the one, and then it's game over.'

Mum teased Dad. 'Maybe that explains why they're so angry and miserable all the time.'

He pretended to be outraged. 'What is wrong with you?'

'What is wrong with you?' responded Mum with a giggle. 'You're such a cheeseball!'

Dad leant over and kissed her, which should have been romantic and nice and everything, except ... Penguin was not impressed and didn't like Mum's attention turning elsewhere. She squawked loudly and flew down to their feet, thinking this public display of affection had gone on too long already.

Mum smiled at Penguin. 'You're cold. Come here.'

Penguin flew up into her lap and snuggled there for warmth. Dad rolled his eyes. Bumped for a bird!

*

Mum began spending more and more time training with Gaye. It gave her something to look forward to, and it helped her get fit and strong, which had always been so important to her. Time in nature and in the water made a huge difference to how she felt about the world and herself.

One day Gaye turned up at the house to pick up Mum because Dad was out on a job. It was the first time Gaye and Penguin met each other. And it didn't go well …

Gaye drove a big four-wheel drive up our driveway.

I was listening to music outside and called out, 'Hey, Mum. Gaye's here.'

Mum wheeled herself out the front door a second later. She was all set to go, already wearing her rashie.

Gaye wolf-whistled Mum. 'So, who's ready to —' She saw a magpie in her peripheral vision flying towards her and waved her arms around in panic. 'Whoa! No! Go away! Shoo! Shoo!'

Mum laughed. 'It's okay. This is Penguin.'

Gaye thought Mum had gone mad. 'That's a flippin' magpie, Sam.'

'Her *name's* Penguin,' clarified Mum.

Gaye frowned. 'She's a pet?'

'Well, a companion more than a pet.'

Gaye was not okay with this. 'No, no, no. I don't like maggies. They're evil birds and they can't be trusted.'

I had to intervene at this point. Calling Penguin evil? I don't think so. 'Penguin's okay,' I told Gaye. 'She's a Bloom.'

'A maggie almost killed my brother, you know,' said Gaye.

'*What?*' Mum and I said together.

'Well, it almost blinded him. Came this close to taking out his eye,' she said, showing a tiny gap between two of her fingers. Gaye looked at Penguin with grave distrust. 'You come near me, birdie, I'll take you apart. I'll serve you up with spuds and beans. You got that?'

Penguin may not have known exactly what Gaye was threatening, but she knew it was something bad. She gave Gaye a hard stare.

Mum looked over at me, eyes wide, trying not to laugh at Gaye's over-the-top reaction to Penguin.

A moment later Gaye slapped on her big, friendly smile. 'Right. Let's get going, shall we?'

'Have fun,' I said as Penguin landed on my shoulder, staring suspiciously after Gaye as she wheeled Mum towards the car.

CHAPTER 13

A few weeks later, around the time of Mum's birthday, Penguin was almost an adult bird. She was flying perfectly, but was still spending most of her time around us, which was the way we liked it.

The morning of Mum's birthday, my brothers and I were brushing our teeth. Penguin didn't believe in personal space and checked the inside of my mouth after I took out the toothbrush to make sure I'd done an okay job. Then she flew out of the bathroom and into the kitchen, where Dad was preparing a special birthday breakfast for Mum. Rueben, Oli and I snuck outside to the trampoline so we wouldn't get roped in to helping. We knew Dad and Penguin would have everything under control.

As soon as Dad put the tea bag into the mug of hot water, Penguin pulled it out and flew off with the soggy bag in her beak. Dad did not find this very helpful, but he was used to it.

'It's going to be weak tea then, I guess. Boys!'

We jumped off the trampoline and came running inside. With Dad in the lead and Penguin now on his shoulder, we all tumbled into Mum's bedroom. She was lying in bed, asleep, until we all yelled, 'Happy birthday!'

We tugged on party poppers and coloured paper flew all over the room, which made Penguin squawk. Dad placed the tray in front of Mum.

'Thanks, guys! Wow. Look at all this,' said Mum, smiling happily.

Penguin swooped down from Dad's shoulder and landed next to Mum, kissing her on the cheek.

'Ah, my Penguin,' she said affectionately.

Dad laughed. 'Do you remember it wasn't too long ago it was more like "Get that bird out of the house now"?'

Mum looked innocently at Dad. 'I never said that.' She turned to Penguin. 'Don't listen to him.'

Oli and Rueben crawled into bed beside Mum and hugged and kissed her. I stayed back, watching Mum tickle and cuddle my little brothers.

One of our family traditions is on Mum's birthday, every family member gets measured to see how much they've grown since last year. Mum in her wheelchair leant against the white door edge as Rueben used a dark marker to record her new height on it.

Rueben was mock concerned. 'It looks like you've shrunk, Mum.' He giggled as he wrote *Mum* next to her height.

Oli was next, but he was wearing a pair of Mum's old high heels, so he was disqualified.

'Oh, you cheater.' Mum laughed. 'Don't forget Penguin,' she added. So Penguin had to stand against the wall and get her height taken as well. Oli used the marker, drew the line and wrote *Penguin* there. This made her an official family member.

Later, in my room, I was working on the video diary I'd started soon after Mum came home from the hospital. I hadn't told anyone about it and didn't want to. It was just something that had kinda helped me make sense of everything.

I was doing my voiceover while filming a line of framed family photos that lay on the carpet, using Dad's digital video camera. Some of the photo frames were cracked, others had been stuck back together with tape.

'Mum loves the ocean. She always has. Mum met Dad on the —' I hadn't realised the door was open, and all of a sudden the mum I was talking about was right there in the doorway.

'Hey, what are you doing?' Mum asked. She saw the camera in my hand. And the photos on the carpet. How long had she been there?

I swiftly closed the camera. 'Ah, nothing. It's just a thing,' I said, not making eye contact.

Mum looked concerned. 'What sort of thing?'

I wasn't about to explain what I was doing. 'I can pack these up.'

'Do you need any —? I can help if you like,' said Mum.

'No, it's fine,' I said quickly, turning my back to her. I began packing the photos away.

Mum wasn't sure what to make of my behaviour. 'Well, okay then. We'll be leaving for Nana Jan's in a moment, so make sure you're ready,' she said with a frown, before wheeling herself away.

'Yeah,' I said, shutting the door once she'd left.

CHAPTER 14

The birthday celebrations continued as we went to Nana Jan's for lunch. She lived in an apartment on the third floor of a block of flats. It was a nice place, just like you'd expect a nana's home to be. There were big, soft sofas and lots of ornaments and a large window behind the dining table where Nana could watch the world go by.

She was thrilled to see us and gave everyone hugs and kisses. Then Penguin flew in through the front door over the top of us like she owned the place.

'Oh, you brought Penguin. How nice,' Nana said, when it was clear she didn't mean it at all. We didn't mind because that was just the way Nana was.

It didn't take Penguin long to find a comfortable perch on Nana Jan's favourite light fitting in the living room, the chandelier. When Aunty Kylie arrived and handed over a birthday present, Penguin kept an eye on all of us from above, happily warbling as Mum opened it.

After ripping off the packaging, Mum lifted up a red T-shirt that said *I'm in it for the Parking* and had a handicap sign on it.

Mum grinned. 'Thanks, Kyles.'

'Oh, Sammy. You are so flippin' old,' said Aunty Kylie with a smile.

Mum laughed. 'Huh! I'll wear it well.'

'And I got you bubbles as well.' Aunty Kylie grinned cheekily. 'I only got the cheap stuff though, seeing as you can't taste it.'

'Oh, keep it coming, Kyles!' Mum laughed, never upset with her sister's offbeat sense of humour, even though the rest of us were.

They shared a hug as Nana Jan bustled through the living room. 'Kylie, that table isn't going to set itself, and make sure we use the good napkins,' she instructed, before giving Mum another birthday hug. 'I have waited over a year for the chance for us to all be together like this.'

Unfortunately the nice moment was interrupted by Penguin, who picked right then to poop. Worse still, Nana Jan noticed.

'Oh! Penguin has just pooped on the coffee table. I swear that bird does it just to annoy me.'

Aunty Kylie and Mum laughed as Nana vigorously wiped up the poop with a cloth. Penguin watched her clean, a little bit insulted she was drawing attention to it. Obviously pooping was natural. What was the big deal, Nana Jan?

Nana could tell she was being watched and judged by our magpie. 'Do you have to be inside?' she asked Penguin as the doorbell rang.

'I'll get it,' said Rueben, running down the hall to the door.

Penguin wasn't going to stand for this kind of disrespect from Nana Jan a moment longer, and she took flight, swooping away from the living room and towards the front door just as Rueben opened it.

A second later there was a blood-curdling scream, followed by a *'Shoo, shoo. Get away, you annoying bird!'*

Mum giggled. 'That'll be Gaye.'

After Aunty Kylie had set the table with the nice napkins and the nice glassware and the nice cutlery from the nice sideboard, we all sat down for a meal together. It was delicious. Nana Jan had gone to a lot of effort to make Mum happy on her birthday. And us boys tried our hardest to be on our best behaviour.

Penguin was busy on ground surveillance, hopping around under the dinner table, making sure crumbs and fallen scraps were picked up and eaten as quickly as possible. Gaye could not relax when Penguin got too close to her feet — she had to stifle a couple of squeals when she felt a magpie wing touch her leg — but she tried her best to act as though having a magpie at the table while she was eating was perfectly normal. It made my brothers and me chuckle all the way through the meal.

'So you think Sam's got a shot at competing seriously?' Dad asked Gaye. Really, I think he was just trying to distract her from Penguin.

'Oh yeah,' said Gaye, eyes sparkling.

Nana Jan turned to Aunty Kylie. 'Did you know about this?'

Aunty Kylie laughed. 'Everyone knows about it, Mum, and Sam told you like five times.'

Nana frowned. 'I thought it was just another one of those physio things.'

Gaye went on to explain. 'It's a competition, Jan. Champion potential, this one,' she said, smiling at Mum.

'Are you sure you're up to that?' Nana asked Mum.

Mum knew this conversation was likely to set Nana off. 'It's fine, Mum,' she said soothingly.

But Nana continued, concerned. 'So Sam'll be spending a lot of time in the water?'

Gaye nodded enthusiastically. 'Yep. Training. At least three times a week.'

'It sounds dangerous,' said Nana. 'And Sam can't swim. Can you?'

'Don't you worry, Jan,' said Gaye. 'I haven't drowned a student yet. Now my ex-husband ... Well, that is a whole other story.'

Nana didn't even crack a smile at Gaye's joke. 'Noah, could you grab some more bread from the kitchen please, darling?' she asked.

I went out to the kitchen and saw that Penguin was hopping around, looking through the glass sliding door at the balcony. She wanted to go outside, and as Nana Jan got more stressed about Mum entering kayaking competitions, I was thinking I'd prefer to be outside too. So I opened the door for her. 'There you go, Peng. Some fresh air.'

Penguin walked out onto the balcony and pecked around the pot plants, looking for grubs. She seemed happy there, so I left her to it and returned to the table with the extra bread.

Mum and Nana Jan's conversation continued. 'To be honest, it's the first time I've felt normal since the accident,' explained Mum. 'When I'm kayaking, I look like everyone else.'

'Well, thank goodness for Gaye.' Nana smiled. 'Someone's getting Sam out of the house. Being proactive.'

Nana had gone from stressing about one thing straight into stressing about another.

Aunty Kylie tried to defend Dad. 'Mum, c'mon, that's ... Well, what do you think Cam does all day?'

'That's not what I'm saying, Cam. I didn't mean that.'

'I know,' said Dad kindly.

But that didn't stop Nana. 'I'm only saying it's very hard. You've got your work. Sam's often alone.'

Oli piped up. 'She's not alone. She has Penguin.'

'That's right, bub.' Mum smiled.

Dad continued. 'You know she likes her independence, Jan. Values it a lot.'

'But she can't walk,' said Nana.

Mum was losing patience a bit by this stage. 'Mum, I'm right here.'

'How much independence should she have?' persisted Nana.

'Mum. I'm sitting three feet away from you,' said Mum through gritted teeth.

'But really.'

'Please,' said Mum.

'What if something was to happen?' blurted out Nana.

Dad was also losing patience. 'She has her phone, Jan. She'd call me.'

But Nana was on a roll and just wouldn't stop talking. 'What if she fell? If there was a fire?'

Mum realised us boys shouldn't be listening to this conversation and spoke over Nana Jan. 'Why don't you guys jump in the pool? Roo? Snow? Oli? We'll have the cake afterwards, okay?'

We were happy to leave the adults to fight amongst themselves and quickly cleared our plates off the table. Out on the balcony, Penguin jumped up onto the railing and looked out at the view. Aunty Kylie told me later the 'discussion' got even more tense after we'd left to get changed.

Nana Jan just didn't let up. 'What if Sam was alone and couldn't reach the phone? What if she could reach the phone and it wasn't charged?'

Dad leant in to Nana. 'We don't talk in what-ifs. We live our life.'

'Oh yes. All fun, no responsibility. And look where that's got you.'

There was a gasp from the family still seated at the table. Gaye immediately stood up, not wanting to be a part of this conversation any longer. 'Ah, I might have a swim too,' she said.

But she wasn't allowed to leave. 'Sit down please, Gaye,' said Dad. 'Jan, if you're implying —'

Mum shook her head. 'She's not implying anything, Cam. She's just drunk and emotional.'

Nana Jan got defensive. 'I heard that.'

'Of course you did. You're three feet away!'

Nana wasn't finished yet. 'When your poor father died —'

Aunty Kylie groaned. 'Not this again,' she muttered.

Gaye made another attempt to leave the table. But was stopped once again.

'Sit please, Gaye,' Mum and Dad said in unison.

Gaye sat.

Nana continued, almost sobbing now. 'When your poor father died,' she started again, 'I thought, "At least I've still got my girls." Now I lie awake every night and worry.'

'And I don't?! All I ever do is worry,' said Dad.

Mum tried to stop Dad, but he was not going to be stopped now. 'I worry if I'm too happy around Sam or too sad around the boys. I worry if I should take them to the beach or if that's us being selfish. I worry if I'm doing too much or not enough.'

'I know,' said Nana with a sob.

'I worry Sam can't walk because I moved her after she fell,' blurted out Dad.

Mum wasn't happy about that. 'Cam, no. The doctors said that had nothing to —'

'Believe me, Jan, I worry,' finished up Dad.

'I know you worry, love. I'm sorry,' said Nana, finally realising she'd really upset Dad. 'I'm just scared. I just wish I could make my little girl better, but I can't. And it makes me crazy. But I —'

Mum had tuned out of the conversation and was listening in to something outside. '*Ssshh*,' she said to Nana Jan.

Nana did not like to be shushed. 'Don't you shush me, Sam,' she said, a bit tired and emotional.

Mum's face turned to the window. There was an alarmed squawk. 'Did you hear that?' she asked her family and Gaye.

'What?' asked Dad.

Suddenly they all heard a loud, pained SQUAWK! Dad ran to the balcony and looked down. There was Penguin on the ground, being attacked by two other larger magpies. There was screeching and scratching as the birds jumped on little Penguin. 'Get out of it!' yelled Dad.

Mum could see what was going on from her place at the dining table, and she banged on the window pane, trying to scare the magpies off Penguin, but they kept attacking her. 'Stop it! Penguin!'

By that stage my brothers and I had rushed over and looked past the balcony rail to see poor Penguin. 'Penguin!' we yelled. It was so awful to see our little friend getting savaged.

Dad sprinted through the apartment to head downstairs. Mum was still by the window, shouting, 'Get off her! Cam, stop them!'

The hostile magpies kept attacking Penguin. She tried to defend herself, but the life she had lived with us had not prepared her for the harsh realities of the outside world. She was struggling as the two bullies pecked and prodded her with their beaks and claws.

'Leave her alone!' yelled Mum.

Dad finally got to the backyard and scared off the birds. 'Get outta here!' he shouted.

The attacking magpies squawked with fury as they left.

Before Dad could get to Penguin, bloody and dazed from the brutal attack, she took flight in the opposite direction to the other birds.

Mum was yelling, 'Penguin, no!' but she flew off shakily.

We all watched Penguin fly away from us, hurt and terrified, and no matter how loud we called to her, there was soon no sign of her.

Mum and I shared a look, devastated that poor little Peng had gone.

CHAPTER 15

We stayed at Nana Jan's for a while, hoping Penguin would return. Dad dropped Mum back at home just in case Penguin turned up there. Rueben, Oli, Aunty Kylie and I went out with Dad once he came back, walking the streets, calling and calling for Peng. And to top it off, a storm was brewing. Moments later large droplets fell from the sky. We were drenched in seconds, but it didn't stop us from looking for our Penguin.

Nana came out with a big umbrella for us. 'I knew it. Not an umbrella amongst you,' she said, tut-tutting at the sight of us all sopping wet.

'We're about to head home,' said Dad. 'No point continuing in this weather.'

But I didn't want to give up. 'Maybe she's at the beach?' I asked.

'It's getting dark, Snow,' replied Dad.

'Five more minutes,' I pleaded.

Nana was fussing. 'Look at you in your wet clothes. You're all going to get sick.'

Dad sighed. 'Let's give them another five minutes more. Off you go, boys. Quickly.'

Rueben and I ran off, calling out for Penguin.

Dad picked up Oli, who looked exhausted and red-eyed from crying. 'Why did they do it, Dad? Penguin wouldn't hurt anyone.'

Dad tried to explain. 'Magpies are territorial, mate. Technically this isn't Penguin's home, it's theirs. They were only defending their home.'

That explanation didn't make either of them feel any better. Penguin hadn't deserved to be beaten up like that. She'd done nothing wrong.

Oli buried his face into Dad's neck. 'But we're Penguin's home,' he sobbed.

Dad was heartbroken. 'I know, Oli, I know.'

*

Back at our house, Mum sat by the living room window, staring into the night as the storm raged outside. She was trying to catch a glimpse of a wing, or the sound of a familiar squawk, but it was only the sounds of the storm rattling the windows that caught her attention.

She wheeled her chair around the house, restless and annoyed she couldn't be outside with us, helping to look for Penguin. She entered my room, noticing Penguin's basket. Mr Murphy the monkey stared back at her, forlorn and weathered.

I'd left my laptop on, and Mum was still curious about what I'd been doing with the broken photo frames and the video camera earlier in the day. So she tapped a key to remove the screen saver, and a photo of her in the bus in Thailand appeared. She didn't usually snoop on us at all, but she wanted to know what was going on in my head. And she didn't think she could ask me directly. If she had, I wouldn't have been able to say. Not really. So Mum pressed play, and she saw pictures of herself and the hotel we stayed in, the viewing platform where she fell, and her injuries during her many hospital visits. And she heard my voiceover:

... other days it could have broken, but it waited for Mum. And I'm the one who took her there. I wish it was me that leant on that fence. I wish it was me that broke my back.

And although I didn't want her to hear it like that, or look at my laptop when I wasn't there, it was true. I was able to say on video what I couldn't say to anyone around me, not to my dad, my brothers and especially not to Mum.

Mum was shocked and upset by what she'd heard on my laptop. She shut the computer back down and wheeled herself out of my room when our car arrived outside, hoping for good news.

But we didn't have any good news for her. Penguin was still missing.

CHAPTER 16

We all felt miserable as Mum tucked Oli into bed later that night. Fireworks started to light up the sky.

'Is it New Year's Eve?' Oli asked Mum.

'No.'

'Then why are there fireworks?' asked Oli.

Mum shrugged. 'I don't know. Sometimes nice things just happen.'

Rueben turned up at Oli's bedroom door in his pyjamas. He had something to say to Mum and he wasn't going to sleep until he'd said it.

'Are you mad at Noah?' he asked bravely.

Mum was surprised by the question. 'Of course not.'

Rueben continued, not sure he believed Mum's statement. 'Because anyone could've let Penguin out onto the balcony at Nana's.'

'I know,' said Mum.

Rueben looked at her a moment longer, nodded and went back to his bedroom.

Unaware of my brothers' conversations with Mum until later, I was up on the roof with a flashlight, calling out Penguin's name. There was no way I was ready to sleep.

The fireworks felt so wrong. With Penguin gone, there was nothing in the world worth celebrating, and I hated the idea of people enjoying themselves when Penguin was out there, alone and hurt.

I eventually went to bed, but woke up early the next morning and biked down to the beach, searching for Penguin. I went to the spot where I'd found her as a tiny chick, months earlier, when she'd fallen from the Norfolk pine. I knew she probably wouldn't have remembered that was once her home, but I couldn't think of where else she might have gone.

She wasn't there either.

When I got home, the rest of the family were already in the living room, looking glum. They could tell by the way I walked inside I hadn't found her at the beach.

I went and stared out the window.

'You alright, Snow?' asked Dad.

I didn't answer. Or even turn my head away from the window. I wasn't alright.

'Do you think she's dead?' asked Rueben.

'Geez, no. She's just scared,' said Dad. 'Give her time to find her way home. She knows where we are. And Penguin's tough. Isn't that right, Sammy?'

Mum didn't reply, but I could feel her staring at me. 'Noah,' she said.

I kept silent.

'He's okay. He's just —' started Dad, but Mum interrupted him.

'Noah, it's not your fault,' she said sharply.

Dad agreed with Mum immediately. 'Of course it's not your fault.'

Mum continued. 'You've got to stop this, Snow. You've got to let it go.'

Dad wasn't sure what was going on. 'Right. Ah, what?'

'You're not to blame for Penguin being attacked, Noah, and you're not to blame for my accident,' Mum carried on.

'Whoa, whoa, okay, let's not turn this into something it's not. No-one's saying he is. Let's just —' said Dad, trying to troubleshoot, but Mum wasn't going to be stopped.

'*He* thinks he is responsible for my accident,' she said, her breath catching in her throat. 'Don't you, Noah?'

'Why do we have to talk about this?' I asked, upset.

'Because I'm tired of *not* talking about it,' answered Mum.

I started to leave the living room.

'Honey, don't walk away! Listen to me!' shouted Mum.

I stopped and turned around, speaking quietly. 'You say I'm not to blame, Mum, but you don't mean it.'

Dad really wasn't sure what was going on between the two of us. 'Of course she means it, Snow.'

I was sick of him trying to make things better. 'You don't know anything, Dad!' I yelled.

'Hey, that's enough,' he said.

'You don't see the way she looks at me!' My voice was still raised.

'Inside voice, mate,' said Dad.

But Mum intervened at that point. 'Shut up, Cam! Since when have we been an inside-voice family? We used to scream our heads off. That's what families do. I'm fed up with tiptoeing around every single word. Please, Noah, if you've got something to say, just say it.'

Rueben and Oli were watching this fight play out, mouths open in surprise, not saying a thing. I had always been the calm one, the quiet one, the responsible older brother. It was always Rueben and Oli shouting, never me. And now they could see how upset I was, and no-one really knew what was going to happen next. Including me!

'No,' I said stubbornly.

'I need you to talk to me,' said Mum angrily. '*Please. Please.*'

I couldn't keep quiet any longer. It was like a dam burst inside me. 'It was my fault we went up that tower in Thailand! It was my idea! I'm the reason you broke your back and that you can't walk! Are you happy?' I cried.

'No! I'm not happy!' Mum yelled back at me.

'And sometimes I think I'll never be happy again. But that is not because of you!'

'Then why don't you ever want to talk to me? Or — or be near me?'

'I-I don't know,' she stumbled.

'You hug Oli all the time! You can't even look at me,' I said.

'I've made lots of mistakes, Snow,' said Mum, no longer yelling. 'I'm terrified all this anger will come spewing out of me. Not just at you. At all of you. At you, Cam. And I wish … Every day I wish we never went onto that platform. But we went. And that was our decision, not yours. You're not to blame for any of it, Noah. It was just an old piece of rotten wood that gave way.'

We were all listening hard. Mum had never spoken about the accident like this before, and I think the rest of us held our breath as she continued.

'But I'm sorry I haven't been strong enough to help you understand that. Or to help you through

133

it. Any of you. I didn't think I'd have the strength to get myself through it. But I do. I know that now. I'm here. I'm your mum. The same mum,' she said as she opened her arms. 'Just give me a chance to prove it.'

That was the invitation I'd been waiting months for, and I ran into her arms, sobbing. And the same mum, my favourite mum, gave me the best hug of my life.

There was no way Oli was going to miss out on a hug this good. He rushed over and joined the hug. And then Rueben did, of course, and then Dad …

As I continued to be smothered by my family's hugs, I realised it had felt good to at last say what I'd been thinking silently for so long. It felt even better to hear Mum say she didn't blame me for her fall. It was the biggest relief to hear her explain it in a way I understood to be true. I knew when I went back to my room that I'd delete my video diary. I didn't need it anymore. It wasn't the right story, and it wasn't the truth. I had thought it was, but I'd been wrong. And I was really, really happy to be wrong.

As we finally untangled ourselves from each other, tears dripping down our faces, there was a moment of calm. We didn't have Penguin, but at least the Blooms felt like a complete family again, like we were all on the same side, and we could support one another while we hoped for our feathered friend's return.

CHAPTER 17

As the days went on, Mum started kayaking more and more, getting ready for her first big competition. And it made her happy, so we felt happier too. I'd still go up to the roof every day after school and scan the skies for Penguin. It just wasn't the same without her. One day, to prove to myself I could, I even did Rueben's trick of jumping off the roof onto the trampoline. It felt good. Like flying. So I did it another three times. Imagine what flying like a magpie must feel like? Amazing.

Yeah, Penguin was never far from my mind.

Mum and I were getting on better, and she had as many hugs for me now as she did for my brothers. She knew how much I was missing Penguin because she was too. I saw her smile sadly when she had to pull the tea bag out of her own tea in the morning. It was one of Penguin's favourite jobs.

A few weeks after the fight at Nana Jan's, to distract us all from missing Penguin, Dad decided to give Mum a big surprise. It took quite a bit of organisation, but Dad loved a project, and this was a special one.

Dad grinned from ear to ear as he put a blindfold over Mum's eyes while she waited in the living room.

'Oh, okay then. I give up. What's this all about?' asked Mum with a hesitant smile.

'We're going out,' I said.

Dad added, 'We're not spending another night staring at Penguin's basket. We're going out for fish and chips.'

'And I need a blindfold on to go to the beach?' asked Mum.

'Who said anything about the beach?' said Dad. 'Are you ready, boys?'

Oli, Rueben and I helped wheel Mum out of the house.

'What exactly are you all up to?' asked Mum, bewildered.

We gave her a countdown ('*Three ... two ... one ... Surprise!*') and Dad whipped off her blindfold.

In the driveway, leaning against the hood of her four-wheel drive, was Mum's coach, Gaye. She gave Mum a thumbs-up.

'Oh. It's just Gaye,' said Mum, not understanding what was going on at all yet.

Gaye was also in on our surprise. 'It is not just Gaye,' she said sternly. 'It is Gaye and ... Gaye's truck.'

Gaye gestured behind her. The four-wheel drive had a large dropcloth draped over the roof, hiding something bulky. From behind the vehicle sprang Mum's best friend, Bron, Aunty Kylie and Nana Jan. 'Surprise!' yelled Bron.

'What ...?' said Mum, still not having a clue what was happening.

'Don't look at me, Sam. No-one tells me anything,' said Nana Jan in typical fashion.

'What is going on?' Mum asked.

Meanwhile, Dad had walked over to the four-wheel drive and was pulling the dropcloth off to reveal ... 'Your chariot awaits,' he said with a flourish.

We had helped Dad build a special seat for Mum. It was made out of an old foldaway deck chair that we'd attached to two kayak paddles and roped together. It was like one of those thrones that kings in Ancient Rome were carried around on by all their servants. Or was it Ancient Greece? Who knows. Anyway, you get the idea. It was not what Mum was expecting at all.

'Ah, what is that?' she asked, smiling but bemused.

'I told you. We're going out for fish and chips,' said Dad, and he pointed towards Barrenjoey Lighthouse, the one place Mum had not been able to visit since her accident. The path up there was not made for wheelchairs, and it was a place Dad knew she dreamed of visiting.

'But only if you want to?' he added with a grin.

Mum thought for a moment and nodded, smiling. Her grateful expression was the answer Dad was after.

So we took a couple of vehicles and drove to the base of the lighthouse path. Dad carefully moved Mum from the car into her chariot. There was quite a bit of giggling at the start of the trek, because it turned out an old foldaway chair wasn't the most stable seat we could have chosen for the chariot, but Mum didn't complain. The kayak paddles were held by Dad, Gaye, Bron and Aunty Kylie, but the laughing subsided when we began the ascent to the lighthouse. It was hard work for the chair lifters, but like the great coach she was, Gaye was there to cheer them on.

'Okay, drive. And driiiiive, baby!' she repeated at regular intervals, making us all break out into giggles again.

I challenged Rueben to an uphill running race and managed to keep him from overtaking me as we sprinted towards the summit.

Mum kept silent and just watched the landscape from her chair, enjoying every second of the climb she didn't think she'd ever get the chance to do again.

The path moved deeper into bush as we neared the top of Barrenjoey Point, the most northern point of Sydney. And then we were at the summit. The lighthouse stood there, waiting for us. It was sturdy and dependable, built with sandstone one hundred and twenty years ago, and most importantly, a place

Mum had loved spending time from back when she was a young girl. She said she could hear the sounds of nature best from here. There was the roar of the surf below; the birds in the trees behind her, all singing their different songs; the rustle of animals moving; and if she was by herself, she could even hear her own heartbeat. She said she felt very much a part of the universe at this spot, and any worries she had disappeared when she visited Barrenjoey Point.

We lowered the chair by the edge of the lighthouse so Mum could look out over the vast ocean. Everyone gave her hugs and kisses. We knew how much she appreciated Dad's surprise.

Dad let her admire the view by herself for a few minutes while the rest of us organised the picnic dinner. Then he came up gently behind her and put his hand on her shoulder.

Mum smiled. 'This was all pretty sneaky, Cam.'

Dad smiled too. 'Yep.' He took her hand and they looked out over the ocean. At the sea birds wheeling above. At a world teeming with life and colour and wonder.

'Ask me that question,' said Mum.

'Which question?'

Mum laughed. 'The one I told you never to ask me.'

Dad took a moment. 'How are you?'

Mum contemplated her answer, and then looked up at Dad. 'I'm … better, thank you, Cam,' she said, kissing him. She looked over at her family, Dad by her side, realising how far she'd come with support from the people she loved.

CHAPTER 18

Of course, what goes up must come down, and after a picnic at the Point, we bundled everything into backpacks, hoisted Mum into her chair and set off back down the track to the cars.

By the time we were almost home, it was dusk and we were tired but happy. It had been a successful trip. As Dad pulled into the driveway, I heard something. I wound down the window and looked up. It was a magpie's call. Mum was listening too.

'Could be another one,' she said, trying not to get her hopes up.

But I knew Penguin's song. 'It's not, Mum. It's not.'

Dad turned off the engine and I stumbled out of the car as fast as I could, running towards the frangipani tree. And there she was!

Penguin!

Perched on one of the lower branches, waiting for us like she'd never been away.

'Hi, Peng.'

I yelled back to the others, 'It's Penguin! She's back!' I gave her a cuddle and a kiss while Rueben and Oli ran up behind me.

'Penguin, Penguin, Penguin!' cried Oli, who a moment ago had almost been asleep in the car.

'About time, Peng!' shouted Rueben, who pretended to be more chill than the rest of us, but he was as pleased to see her as we were.

Penguin chirped happily as us boys crowded around her, taking turns patting her.

By that stage Dad had got Mum out of the car and into her wheelchair. Penguin looked past us and saw Mum watching her, with tears in her eyes. Penguin flew over our heads and landed on Mum's lap. Mum cried with happiness, burying her face in Penguin's feathers.

That night was one of the best we'd had in a while, with *all* the family back together again. Mum made popcorn, we watched a movie, and Penguin was never far away, landing on Oli's head, picking fluff from my shirt, helping Mum with tea-bag removal, flying around the living room like she owned the place. She hadn't forgotten a thing. She was very happy to see Mr Murphy in her basket, waiting for her. She gave him a loving peck, but she didn't spend too long away from where she belonged, which was Mum's lap.

A few days after Penguin returned home, she was hanging out with Mum in the living room. My brothers and I were at school, and Dad had gone out to a photography job in the city. Mum was busy putting some old photos into new frames. These were the photos she'd knocked down when she was angry with the world, the ones that showed her life before the accident. Now she was happier, she was ready to look at them again.

Mum told us later that Penguin watched her closely, and once the old photos had been rehung, Mum added new photos to the collection. There were recent photos taken by Dad of her and Penguin, and of us boys, and of Mum paddling in the kayak. There was even one of our favourites: a photo of Mum and Penguin lifting weights together. It was obviously one of Penguin's favourite photos as well, because she chirped happily to see Mum mount it on the wall.

Mum laughed. 'You like that one, huh?'

Then Penguin stopped keeping an eye on Mum and the photos and flew away, finding Mr Murphy in the laundry basket and dragging him across the floor.

Mum stopped what she was doing and looked at Penguin, who continued to take Mr Murphy down the hall. A moment later they disappeared into my bedroom.

Mum wheeled herself to my room. And there she found Penguin dragging Mr Murphy onto my bed. Mum said nothing as she watched the magpie lay Mr Murphy carefully on my pillow. Then Penguin hopped onto the open windowsill and flew outside.

Mum looked back at the monkey on my bed and a strange feeling came over her. So she quickly manoeuvred herself out of the bedroom, back up the hall and out the front door into the yard.

Penguin was there, perched in her frangipani tree, and it looked like she was waiting for Mum.

'What are you up to, Penguin?' Mum asked. In her heart, she already knew the answer.

Penguin looked back at Mum for a few seconds, and Mum could feel the connection they had. And she knew this was Penguin telling her it was time to say goodbye.

That was why Penguin had returned Mr Murphy to my bed, and that was why she visited the frangipani tree one last time.

Penguin jumped across to Mum's lap and rubbed her head across Mum's hands, which was a proper magpie hug. Mum picked up Penguin and pressed a kiss onto her head.

Penguin gave Mum one last loving look, and then turned her face to the sky.

Mum was so proud of this beautiful bird and grateful for what she'd done for our family. 'Penguin. Thank you,' she said.

Penguin shifted her body and took flight. Mum watched her sail over the trees and towards the ocean, until she was just a black and white speck in the sky.

*

So this is the story that I wanted to tell you. There were bits that weren't easy to talk about, but like

I said in the beginning, it's a story that needed to be told. Because sometimes bad things happen to people. And maybe people think that's the story you need to hear. But it isn't. The story that matters, really matters, is how we respond when bad things happen, and what we need to get us through tough times.

Penguin never returned to our house. Of course we never knew where she had gone in the weeks after her fight at Nana Jan's, and we'd never know, but Penguin had healed without our help, and she seemed less like the little bird that had once desperately needed us to survive. She was more grown-up and independent. Which was always what we'd wanted for her. We loved having her around, but she wasn't ever our pet. We knew that. She deserved to live her life the way a magpie did. In the wild. And perhaps one day she would start a family of her own. But wherever she went, she was always going to be a part of the Bloom family.

Mum went on to win two national kayaking championships and competed at the World Championships in Italy. And then later became a two-time World Adaptive Surfing Champion.

I'm incredibly proud of my mum. She's no longer the person she once was and I know she's not the person she wanted to be, but to me, she's become much more than that.

I'm so grateful that Penguin came into our lives when she did. Some things can seem beyond fixing, but in our case, something like a baby magpie falling out of a nest during a storm can start a chain of events that helps you to heal and love life all over again.

That's a story worth telling, don't you think?